QUOTES AND IMAGES FROM THE MEMOIRS OF CASANOVA

Jacques Casanova de Seingalt

[ZHINGOORA BOOKS]

The Memoirs of

CASANOVA

Venetian Years

The Memoirs of

CASANOVA

Paris and Prison.

The Memoirs of

CASANOVA

In London and Moscow

The Memoirs of

CASANOVA

Adventures in the South

A man never argues well except when his purse is well filled

Accepted the compliment for what it was worth

Accomplice of the slanderer

Advantages of a great sorrow is that nothing else seems painful

Age, that cruel and unavoidable disease

All women, dear Leah are for sale

All-powerful lever, gold

Alms given in public are sure to be

accompanied by vanity

Anger and reason do not belong to the
same family

Angry man always thinks himself right

At my age I could not be allowed to
have any opinions

Augurs could never look at each other
without laughing

Awkward or miserly, and therefore
unworthy of love

Axiom that "neglected right is lost
right"

Beauty is the only unpardonable offence

in your eyes

Beauty without wit offers love nothing

Bed is a capital place to get an

appetite

Best plan in this world is to be

astonished at nothing

Beware of the man of one book

Calumnies are easy to utter but hard to

refute

Cherishing my grief

Clever man deceives by telling the
truth

Commissaries of Chastity

Confession

Contempt of life

Could tell a good story without
laughing

Criticism only grazed the skin and
never wounded deeply

Delights are in proportion to the
privations we have suffered

Desire is only kept alive by being

denied

Desire to make a great fuss like a

great man

Despair which is not without some

sweetness

Despised ignoramus becomes an enemy

Diminish the tale of your years instead

of increasing it

Distance is relative

Divinities—novelty and singularity

Do not mind people believing anything,

provided it is not true

Do their duty, and to live in peace and

sweet ignorance

Economy in pleasure is not to my taste

Emotion is infectious

Essence of freedom consists in thinking

you have it

Everything hung from an if

Exercise their reason to avoid the

misfortunes which they fear

Fanaticism, no matter of what nature,

is only the plague

Fatal desire for luxury and empty show

spoils all

Favourite passion has always been

vengeance

First motive is always self-interest

Foolish enough to write the truth

For in the night, you know, all cats

are grey

For is love anything else than a kind

of curiosity?

Fortune flouts old age

Found him greater at a distance than
close at hand

Gave the Cardinal de Rohan the famous
necklace

Girl who gave nothing must take nothing

Give yourself up to whatever fate
offers to you,

Government ought never to destroy
ancient customs abruptly

Groans, and prayers, and blasphemies

Happiness is purely a creature of the
imagination

Happiness is not lasting—nor is man

Happy or unhappy from a merely cursory
inspection

Happy ignorance!

Happy age when one's inexperience is
one's sole misfortune

Hasty verses are apt to sacrifice wit
to rhyme

He won't be uneasy—he is a philosopher

Hobbes: of two evils choose the least

Honest old man will not believe in the
existence of rascals

Idle questions which are commonly
addressed to a traveller

If this and if that, and every other if

If I could live my life over again

If history did not lie

Ignorance is bliss

Ignorant, who talk about everything

right or wrong

Imagine that what they feel themselves

others must feel

It is only fools who complain

It's too much for honour and too little

for love

Jealousy leads to anger, and anger goes

a long way

Knowing that he would not be regretted

after his death

Last thing which we learn in all

languages is wit

Laugh out of season

Let not thy right hand know what thy
left hand doeth

Lie a sufficient number of times, one
ends by believing it

Light come, light go

Love always makes men selfish

Look on everything we don't possess as
a superfluity

Love fills our minds with idle visions

Love makes no conditions

Made a point of forgetting everything
unpleasant

Made a parade of his Atheism

Man needs so little to console him or
to soothe his grief

Marriage without enjoyment is a thorn
without roses

Marriage state, for which I felt I had
no vocation

Married a rich wife, he repented of

having married at all

Mere beauty does not go for much

Most trifling services are assessed at

the highest rates

My spirit and my desires are as young

as ever

My time was too short to write so

little

Mystical insinuations

Negligent attire

Never to pass an opinion on any subject

Never wearied himself with too much
thinking

Nobody read his books, but everybody
agreed he was learned

'Non' is equal to giving the lie

Now I am too old to begin curing myself

Obscenity disgusts, and never gives
pleasure

Oh! wonderful power of self-delusion

One never knows enough

Owed all its merits to antithesis and

paradox

Pardonable weakness, most of us prefer

"mine" to "thine"

Passing infidelity, but not inconstancy

Passion and prejudice cannot reason

People did not want to know things as

they truly were

People want to know everything, and

they invent

Pigmies mimicking a giant

Pity to sell cheaply what would have to
be replaced dearly

Pleasures are realities, though all too
fleeting

Pope, whom no Roman can believe to be
infallible

Post-masters

Prejudices which had the sanction of
the law

Pride is the daughter of folly

Privately indulged in every luxury that
he forbade to others

Privilege of a nursing mother

Promising everlasting constancy

Proud nation, at once so great and so
little

Quacks

Rather be your debtor than for you to
be mine

Read when I am gone

Reading innumerable follies one finds
written in such places

Repentance for a good deed

Reproached by his wife for the money he
had expended

Rid of our vices more easily than of
our follies

Rome the holy, which thus strives to
make all men pederasts

Rumour is only good to amuse fools

Sad symptom of misery which is called a
yawn

Sadness is a disease which gives the
death-blow to affection

Scold and then forgive

Scrupulously careful not to cheat you
in small things

Seldom praised and never blamed

Selfishness, then, the universal motor
of our actions?

Shewed his contempt by saying nothing

Sin concealed is half pardoned

Sleep—the very likeness of
non-existence

Snatching from poor mortal man the delusions

Soften the hardships of the slow but certain passage to the grave

Stupid servant is more dangerous than a bad one

'Sublata lucerna nullum discrimen inter feminas'

Submissive gaze of a captive who glories in his chain

Surface is always the first to interest

Talent of never appearing to be a

learned man

Taste and feeling

Tell me whether that contempt of life
renders you worthy of it

There is no cure for death

There's time enough for that

Time that is given to enjoyment is
never lost

Time that destroys marble and brass
destroys also the very memory

Time is a great teacher

Timidity is often another word for
stupidity

To know ill is worse than not to know
at all

Vengeance is a divine pleasure

Verses which, like parasites, steal
into a funeral oration

Victims of their good faith

Wash their dirty linen in private

What is love?

When we can feel pity, we love no

longer

When one is in an ill humour,

everything is fuel for the fire

Whims of the mob and the fancies of the

Republic

Wife worthy of being a mistress

Wiser if they were less witty

Wish is father to the thought

Wit cannot stand before stupidity

Woman has in her tears a weapon

Women are always as old as they look

Women would be either tyrants or slaves

Women often do the most idiotic things
out of sheer obstinacy

World of memories, without a present
and without a future

Would like to shape the laws according
to their needs

Wretch treats me so kindly that I love
him more and more

If you wish to read the entire context of any of these quotations, select a short segment and copy it into your clipboard memory—then open the plain text eBook below and paste a small part of the phrase into your computer's find or search operation.

The End

www.ingramcontent.com/pod-product-compliance
Lightning Source LLC
Chambersburg PA
CBHW060020300526
45794CB00003B/1224